MEDITATION

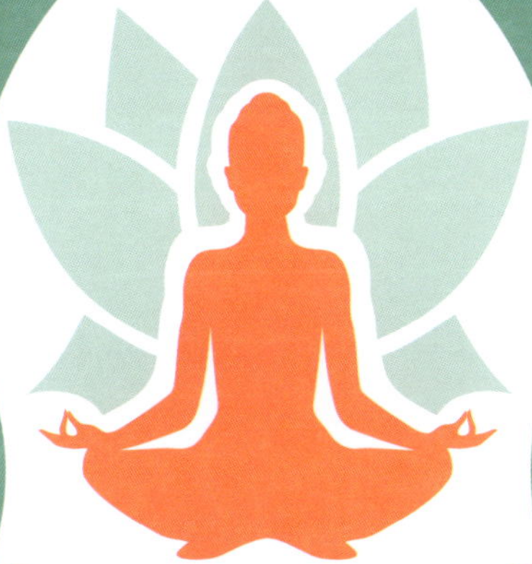

ILLUSTRATED GUIDE

Written by Belinda Campbell

Designed by Simon Parker
Edited by Cameron-Rose Neal

Copyright © 2024 Igloo Books Ltd

Published in 2025
First published in the UK by SparkPool Publishing
An imprint of Igloo Books Ltd
Cottage Farm, NN6 0BJ, UK
Owned by Bonnier Books
Sveavägen 56, Stockholm, Sweden

All rights reserved, including the right of reproduction
in whole or in part in any form.

Manufactured in China. 0625 001
10 9 8 7 6 5 4 3 2 1

ISBN 978-1-83650-136-7
IglooBooks.com
bonnierbooks.co.uk

CONTENTS

Time to Start Your Meditative Journey!....4
What Is Meditation?................................. 8
Getting Started 12
Facing Challenges................................... 20
Meditating With Crystals 26
Incorporating the Elements 30
Meditation Cards..................................... 34
Meditation Dice 40
Meditation Dice Practices 44
Meditation Master 52
Keeping Motivated.................................. 60
Going Further.. 62
Glossary.. 64

TIME TO START YOUR MEDITATIVE JOURNEY!

Meditation is a type of mental training that allows you to find calm in chaos by engaging with the present. Practiced for millennia, meditation has been found to improve mental focus and emotional and physical wellbeing by helping to break bad habits, expand compassion, and boost productivity and creativity. The skill of meditation exists in everyone but can dull without practice, so let this guide act as a whetstone to sharpen those buried instincts and rediscover the present.

Using a combination of mind-body techniques such as breathwork, visualization, mantras, and yoga poses, meditation is a mindfulness practice with endless possibilities. Much more than simply sitting cross-legged for hours in silence, the various ways to meditate mean that the process will look different for everyone but, at its core, meditation challenges you to reflect, contemplate, or focus on one thing at a time to help quiet a busy mind and engage in the present.

During meditation, multiple thoughts and emotions may still pass through you—but try not to fight them. Thoughts and emotions ebb and flow like the tide—they can be calm and still, or crashing and overbearing. Meditation lets you ride the waves and wait out the storms by helping you to accept that thoughts and emotions exist to be acknowledged and felt rather than solved or ignored. Meditation also allows you to rid yourself of thoughts and feelings that are not serving a positive purpose. So, the next time negative thoughts such as *I'm bad at this* or *Why aren't I more* this *and less* that? are demanding your attention, let them in, let them pass, and then let them go within each meditation practice.

HOW TO USE THIS BOOK

Unwrap the gift of being present with the step-by-step meditations in this book and discover how the tools in your kit can help inspire new and evolving practices to suit your needs.

This kit includes a six-sided meditation dice to encourage you to try new practices, 45 meditation cards to guide your personal meditative journey, a clear quartz crystal, and tealight to aid focus and clarity.

THE CARDS ARE COLOR-CODED INTO THREE GROUPS:

YOGA POSES   **TIMINGS**   **AFFIRMATIONS AND ACTIVITIES**

You can mix and match these cards to create a meditation session that combines one, two, or all three card categories to best match your present mood and needs.

The dice displays a symbol on each side that matches a guided meditation included in the book (see page 44). Use the dice to select a spontaneous meditation to help switch things up or experiment further by using the dice and cards together as your confidence in meditation expands. Whether you are new to mindfulness or looking to renew your awareness, explore how this kit can cultivate, reimagine, and motivate your meditation practice.

 **Meditation Dice**

Tealight   **Clear Quartz Crystal**   **Meditation Cards**

SETTING UP YOUR SPACE

DESIGNATE
Imagine how much harder it would be to achieve everyday tasks without the designated space to complete them in—a kitchen for cooking, a bedroom for sleeping, a bathroom for bathing, etc. While a whole room designated for meditation might be unrealistic, an allocated comfy chair by a window, a bench in the backyard, or an empty corner that you can make your own is plenty to provide the dedicated space and focus your meditation practice deserves.

DECORATE
Select key items that will promote relaxation and provide a restful focus for your senses during meditation. Crystals are often used to complement meditation. Accessorize your space with the kit's clear quartz crystal to invite its properties of healing, relaxation, and deep compassion. To amplify relaxation and positivity, choose a plant like aloe vera, lavender, or jade to breathe life and calmness into your meditation space.

DETACH
Can't hear yourself think, let alone find a quiet place or time to meditate? While a dedicated place can help achieve a serene state, meditation can be practiced on a busy train, in a full house, or anywhere else you want to channel some internal peace. Rather than a physical area, focus on preparing your mental space. Detach from your busy environment, observe any external noise without judgment, and mentally drift into an imagined meditative place.

This product includes a tealight candle and references meditation around lit candles and flames. To prevent fire, never leave a burning candle unattended. Do not burn candles on or near anything that can catch fire. Keep away from children and pets. Use a heat-resistant tealight holder or place upon a heat-resistant surface. Do not burn candles in a cluster, always leave at least 10 cm between burning candles. Keep the wax pool free of wick trimmings, matches, and debris at all times.

WHAT IS MEDITATION?

A BRIEF HISTORY OF MEDITATION

Meditation is arguably a practice as old as humankind, with techniques shared from person to person like favorite recipes passed down over the centuries to feed the mind, body, and soul.

The word "meditation" itself has historical roots in two Latin words: meditari, meaning to think or contemplate, and mederi, meaning to heal.

The art of meditation is a practice with a deep history, that can be dated back thousands of years across many faiths and cultures. From its ancient ties to Hinduism and Buddhism to its influence in the counterculture of the swinging '60s and '70s, the benefits of meditation are no longer only reserved for and associated with the spiritual and free-spirited, but are enjoyed by everyone of all beliefs.

The origins of meditation may be ancient, but its relevance remains as important as ever and its popularity is ever growing. With the thousands of meditation apps available—and global companies like Google offering mindfulness programs that incorporate meditation exercises—the benefits of this practice have never been more accessible. Acknowledged and enjoyed worldwide, the ancient art of meditation remains a vital part of how we take care of ourselves and one another in the present day.

WHAT HAPPENS WHILE MEDITATING?

Meditation may feel good, but what good is it really doing? Claims of long-term meditation being an effective brain training technique have been circulated anecdotally for centuries, and now scientists are beginning to explore what exactly happens while we meditate. Numerous scientific findings support the benefits of meditation, however, the studies of Sara Lazar, a neuroscientist at Harvard Medical School, were some of the first to suggest that meditation can train the brain to adapt, change, and grow stronger in as little as eight weeks.

MEDITATION MARVELS:

- **DMN (Default Mode Network):** Part of the brain region responsible for thoughts about the past and future, known as DMN, becomes less active, freeing you from ruminating on things that have or have not happened and allowing you to tune into the present.
- **Insula:** The part of the brain that makes you aware of your bodily senses, called the insula, becomes more active, enhancing your senses to help anchor you in your meditation and better connect with how you feel in the here and now.
- **Hippocampus:** The grey matter in the hippocampus—associated with learning, memory, self-awareness, and compassion—can thicken, helping ward off age-related memory loss and increase compassion to help you become more open-hearted.
- **Amygdala:** The area of the brain that produces fear and anxiety—called the amygdala—shrinks in volume, helping to reduce the flight-or-fight response and improve stress management.

BENEFITS OF MEDITATION

Meditation is a one-size-soothes-all balm thought to provide psychological, physiological, and spiritual benefits that restore the mind, body, and soul.

MENTAL

Giving your mind a moment to rest and relax is perhaps what meditation is best known for, but it can also be used to improve mental functions, such as clarity of thought, concentration, memory, and stress management. Meditation cannot remove stress but it can reduce the negative symptoms associated with stress by improving mental resilience.

PHYSICAL

Meditation not only calms the mind but also relaxes the body, which can then improve bodily functions such as sleep, digestion, the immune system, and blood pressure. The gray matter increase that occurs in the brain with regular long-term meditation also improves sensory and movement function.

SPIRITUAL

Meditation increases self-awareness and improves intuition by encouraging you to step back and see the bigger picture, letting you discover and rediscover what peace, love, and joy mean to you. Meditation can also increase feelings of joy and gratitude by not letting past or future worries steal the enjoyment of the present.

PRACTICE PATIENCE

Some calming benefits might be felt as soon as you tune into your breath or chant a mantra, but most results will be achieved in the long term and only with regular practice. Try not to fixate on any one specific benefit—the ultimate goal is always the meditation itself. Stay present, practice with patience, and the rest will fall into place.

GETTING STARTED

WHAT YOU NEED TO GET STARTED

Though meditation can be done anywhere and without any equipment, you can strengthen your practice by using certain tools like the components included in this kit. Bring healing energy into your meditation with the clear quartz crystal, find balance with the yoga cards in your card deck, and shake up an old practice or find a new one entirely with a simple roll of the meditation dice. Whether today is your first time or your hundredth, these tools are designed to invigorate old practices and inspire new ones for beginners and pros alike.

When you need extra help getting started, try adding the following to your meditation toolkit:

- A meditation cushion or chair for finding comfort in seated positions.
- A blanket to keep yourself warm during longer, stationary meditations.
- A pen and paper for tracking your meditation journey.
- A device to help you keep time.
- A dedicated meditation space—a place that you do not visit or use often can help you to meditate without distractions, connotations, or expectations.
- An open heart and mind—there are no shortcuts in meditation but, with continuous practice, you will see results. So, sit back and enjoy the journey.

BREATHING TECHNIQUES

Breathing is an important mood indicator—quickening when stressed and lengthening when relaxed—and can be used as a direct pathway to return to the present. Mastering breath awareness can help restore calm and can be used as a sole form of meditation or to complement another practice.

TIPS FOR ANY BREATHING EXERCISE:

- Ease into every breathing exercise with care and awareness. Meditating with your breath is not about forcing anything, but finding what feels good.
- Start each exercise in a comfortable, seated position with your eyes open or closed.
- Take the deepest breath you have taken all day before sighing out an exhale.
- Notice your face soften, your shoulders drop, and your breathing settle back into its natural rhythm. You should already be feeling calmer and ready to start meditating.
- Complete a breathing technique that suits your needs, such as reducing stress or finding focus.
- End every practice with a generous inhale through your nose and release any remaining tension held in your body with a soft sigh out through your mouth.
- With time and practice, this conscious way of breathing will become muscle memory and ensure that your meditation is built upon a calm and focused foundation.

BOX BREATHING: A STRESS-BUSTING BREATH

Visualize drawing a two-dimensional square box with your breath. Inhale through your nose for 2 seconds and picture your breath drawing the top line of a box. Gently pause your breath for 2 seconds as you mentally draw the box's second line. Exhale for 2 more seconds through your mouth as you draw the third line. Pause for 2 final seconds as you complete your box. Try building up to holding your breath for 3 and then 4 seconds.

4-7-8 BREATHING: A CONTROLLED BREATH

Make each breath count with this three-step exercise that focuses on making your exhale twice as long as your inhale. Rest the tip of your tongue behind your upper front teeth and inhale through your nose for 4 seconds. Softly hold your breath for 7 seconds (if needed, build up to this number slowly). Let your tongue rest and then calmly exhale with control through your mouth for 8 seconds.

PURSED LIP BREATHING: A LENGTHENING BREATH

The goal behind this exercise is to blow a flame—real or imagined—without extinguishing it. You may use your kit's tealight or visualize a flame. Inhale through your nose and exhale through your mouth through softly pursed lips, keeping your exhale long and measured.

ALTERNATE NOSTRIL BREATHING: A FOCUSED BREATH

Find focus by inhaling through one nostril at a time. Place your thumb over your right nostril and inhale through your left. Pause your breath while moving your thumb away, place your ring finger over your left nostril and exhale through your right. Keep your ring finger over your left nostril and inhale through the right. Pause your breath while moving your ring finger away, return your thumb to your left nostril and exhale through your right. Continue to alternate between each nostril like so.

MEDITATION TIPS FOR BEGINNERS

Start your meditation journey on the right track! From keeping cozy to staying motivated, follow the handy directions below whenever you feel lost on where to begin or go next on your path to the present.

LOCATE YOUR PEACE

Meditation can be practiced anywhere, however, it can be hard to find your inner peace when your outer peace is also missing. A tranquil location will put you in a calmer mindset and allow you to get the most out of your meditation practice. Outdoor spaces can help you to focus on and feel grateful for the beauty of the present. If you are meditating indoors, try to declutter your meditation space to avoid getting distracted by other tasks.

COMFORT IS KEY

Before you start your meditation, take a moment to ensure that you are in a comfortable position. Use cushions for support and blankets to stay warm and cozy during longer practices. Sitting up allows your body to expand and make full use of your breathwork but, if this doesn't work for you, find another relaxing position that still gives your chest room to open out and breathe deeply.

MEDITATIVE MOMENTS

Use meditation to not only manage tough times but to also find moments of joy. Become present in your day by tapping into your breath during simple but joyful activities such as walking the dog, making a cup of tea, or lighting a candle. Finding these mini meditative moments in your daily routine will boost your confidence in meditation and help you to stay motivated and practice on both the good days and the bad.

INTERNAL AWARENESS

Let your internal bodily sensations ground you to the present moment—notice if your stomach feels full or empty, if your heart is beating fast or slowly, or whether your skin is feeling warm or cold. This collection of sensory information is called interoception and taking note of this can help to improve mental health and regulate emotions. Tune into how you feel at the start of each meditation session to help you better understand what your body needs and choose the best-suited practice.

MEDITATION EXPECTATIONS

Meditation is a skill like any other; it requires time and dedication to start noticing the benefits and see results. Some days you might find your way into the present quickly and, other days, you might find only dead ends. The beauty of meditation is in its infinite beginnings. If you notice your mind wandering, try not to become frustrated. Give yourself permission to start over as many times as needed and learn to find comfort in the knowledge that, in meditation, you can always begin again.

HOW LONG SHOULD YOU MEDITATE FOR?

The longest recorded meditation was completed by Swami Vivekananda in 1892, lasting three days. But longer does not mean better in meditation. There are no rules for how long meditations should last and quality is more important than quantity—however, timing exercises can be a useful way to track your progress and observe improvements.

LONGER MEDITATIONS

Explore one of the longer 15- or 30-minute meditation cards first thing in the morning before your day gets too busy. By beginning with a longer morning meditation, you may find that you can quickly and easily tap into the present throughout the rest of your day.

SHORTER MEDITATIONS

The meditation cards that include 1-, 4-, and 10-minute prompts are ideal for topping off your calm throughout a busy or stressful day. Shorter meditations not only provide a quick spiritual pick-me-up whenever you need but also allow you to fit more bursts of meditation into a single day.

TAKE YOUR TIME

Meditation timings are personal to the individual, so try not to compare your practices with anyone else's. Explore a balance of long and short meditations by using all the meditation timing cards to see which works best for you. Consider setting yourself timing challenges, such as adding an extra minute to your practice every day for 30 days, to use time as a motivational tool. Consistency is more important than duration, so focus on finding the right meditations, long or short, to fit your daily schedule.

FACING CHALLENGES

COMMON CHALLENGES

Meditation is not as easy as it may appear and involves more than just sitting still with your eyes closed. Being mindful of some of the common challenges you might face during a meditation session and learning tools and techniques can help you to overcome them.

COMMON CHALLENGES INCLUDE:

Self-criticism: Feeling like you are not meditating well enough or correctly? Try shifting your mindset to a descriptive rather than a prescriptive approach. Remove any preconceptions of what meditation should be like and instead focus on what it is like for you.

Busy mind: A common misconception is that you cannot meditate unless you "clear your mind." But your brain was made to think just as much as your heart was made to beat. The challenge is to notice your thoughts without judgment. Observe the busyness and, when you have activated your awareness, you can begin to sift through which thoughts you want to keep and which to let go of.

Restlessness: Stillness is not an option for all bodies; so, if you need to move—move. Noticing what works for you is as important as learning what does not. Try giving yourself a simple and soothing task to complete, like making a drink. Alternatively, give yourself a physical focus with movement meditation or yoga.

Wandering mind: Think of meditation and your thoughts as friends rather than foes. If your mind continuously wanders, let it. Use meditation as a time to take a long meandering walk with your thoughts and ideas, like two old friends catching up.

Discomfort: Do not force yourself into any yogi contortions that do not feel right. Take time before each practice to get yourself into a comfortable position that allows you to breathe easily, however that looks for your body.

Impatience: Learning something new and making it habitual takes time; whenever you catch yourself becoming impatient or disheartened, remind yourself that what you are doing is not easy and that your best is always good enough.

Challenges in meditation are not only normal but exist to be embraced. Forcing stillness when you are restless, and striving for silence when your thoughts are demanding to be heard could be the source of your struggle. When meditation is feeling hard, try to soften your approach. Often, the best way to overcome a challenge is to take a moment to breathe in, notice the battle, breathe out, and choose not to fight it. Remember that you are never more than a breath away from resetting your mind and refreshing your meditation.

MEDITATION | Facing Challenges

CHOOSING THE RIGHT MEDITATION FOR YOU

Find your meditation match by asking yourself, what do I want to get out of my practice? The answer might change daily, so check in with yourself before each practice to make sure that you are choosing a meditation that serves your needs.

CHOOSE YOUR MEDITATION GOAL

REBALANCE: Learn the benefits of rebalancing with chakra yoga and take a journey through all seven internal energy centers.

CLARITY: Breath awareness meditation offers a chance to reset your outlook by bringing your awareness back to the basics of breathing in and breathing back out.

CONFIDENCE: The more you know, the more confident your meditation will be—so try a new exercise, mantra, or yoga pose by taking a chance with a roll of the meditation dice.

MOTIVATION: Find your meditation mojo with a motivational mantra to help find your calm or prepare you for a big day.

CALMNESS: Chill a burnt-out brain with the calming practice of Vipassana or Reflective Meditation, both used for reducing the symptoms of stress.

FOCUS: Let your intention come into focus with a visualization meditation to help you set goals and remind yourself what matters most to you.

STILLNESS: Although it might sound counterproductive, adding some movement into your meditation with yoga or walking can ease a restless mind, body, and spirit by giving it a physical focus.

ACCEPTANCE: Ditch the "good vibes only" approach and sit with your thoughts as they come and go with a Noting Meditation, also known as Mindfulness Meditation.

MEDITATION | Facing Challenges

MEDITATING WITH CRYSTALS

BOOSTING YOUR MEDITATION WITH CRYSTALS

While you do not need any equipment for meditation, your practice can be enhanced with meditation tools—and crystals are particularly powerful items to combine. Like meditation, crystals are used to improve physical and mental wellbeing by soothing anxiety, enhancing focus, and engaging with the present.

CLEAR QUARTZ

Struggling to clear your mind? Use the clear quartz crystal included in your kit to help you master meditation. The positive aspects of clear quartz help to declutter a busy brain by clearing out negative thoughts and allowing you to focus on the present moment. This amplifying quartz can boost the properties of other crystals when used alongside them—strengthening their benefits.

CRYSTAL CHOICE

Each crystal has a unique energy, so it is important to find ones that match your practice. Before you select your crystals for meditation, consider your goals and intentions.

Choose a crystal with fitting properties (see page 28) that will channel your needs but always keep your clear quartz nearby for amplification.

COMBINE CRYSTALS WITH MEDITATION:

- **Breathwork awareness:** Meditate with an amber, lepidolite, or amethyst crystal—all linked to respiration—to add new life to a breathing exercise (see pages 14-15).
- **Crystal grids:** Magnify intentions by experimenting with adding crystals into your practice with crystal grids (see page 29).
- **Chakra meditation:** Find internal balance by incorporating crystals associated with the chakras into a chakra practice (see page 59).

WHICH CRYSTALS ARE BEST?

BEST CRYSTALS

Amplify an affirmation and magnify your meditation with the below crystal saviors.

- **CLEAR QUARTZ:** Connected to the crown chakra, clear quartz engages a higher consciousness, bringing clarity and spiritual awareness.
- **AMETHYST:** Aligned with the third-eye chakra, the insightful amethyst helps bring concentration and focus to hone a scattered mind with peace and wisdom.
- **TURQUOISE:** Aligned with the throat chakra, the protective turquoise can help you find meaning in mantra meditation and better connect with breath awareness.
- **GREEN AVENTURINE:** Channel compassion with this heart chakra crystal by incorporating it into a loving kindness meditation.
- **TIGER'S EYE:** Perfect for easing self-doubt, this solar plexus chakra stone nurtures self-worth.
- **RED CARNELIAN:** Connected to the burning passions of the sacral chakra, include the fiery carnelian in a candle gazing meditation.
- **RED JASPER:** Quiet negative voices, add some roar to a mantra, and connect to the present with this root chakra-aligned stone.

WORST CRYSTALS

No type of crystal is bad for meditation, but you may want to avoid the below for the following reasons:

- **ENERGIZING:** Crystals like citrine and turquoise are known for their energizing qualities. While these are great for meditations that incorporate movement, it may be best to steer clear of them if you want a more relaxed meditation or if you meditate before sleeping.
- **UNCLEANSED:** Crystals used to repel and absorb negative energy can become blocked and ineffective over time without regular cleansing, such as smudging or washing.
- **NON-ECO:** Mining for crystals can have a negative environmental impact, so buy crystals from reputable sources to ensure only positive energy enters your meditation space.

MEDITATION | Meditating With Crystals

HOW TO MEDITATE WITH CRYSTALS

Strengthen an intention and supercharge the benefits of your clear quartz by meditating with a crystal grid. Crystal grids are created by placing crystals in a grid-like or geometric shape and are used to strengthen focus. Grids can be as intricate or as simple as you like, but a circular crystal grid is thought to be one the most powerful of all the grid shapes.

BENEFITS
Promotes focus, improves spiritual awareness, and strengthens intentions.

HOW TO PRACTICE WITH A CIRCULAR CRYSTAL GRID:
- Choose an intention for your meditation, such as channeling positivity or focus.
- Gather your clear quartz and any other crystals that match your intention. See the previous page for crystal suggestions and their different properties.
- Create your circle, either in a small formation laid out in front of you or one large enough to sit inside.
- Place your clear quartz crystal in the center of the circle. Alternatively, if you are sitting inside the circle, place the quartz in your lap or balance it on your head to activate its associated crown chakra.
- Visualize a clear light from the quartz filling your mind, body, and crystal grid as you take a deep cleansing inhale through your nose.
- As you exhale, speak the mantra:
  I activate this crystal grid to bring [chosen intention] into my meditation.
- Repeat the visualization, imagining the clear quartz light pulsing through your body on your inhale and then repeat the mantra on your exhale.

INCORPORATING THE ELEMENTS

THE FIVE ELEMENTS IN MEDITATION

Encompassing all five elements into meditation helps balance the mind, body, and spirit to create a full-body experience. The five elements in meditation are earth, water, fire, air, and space. Each element relates to a specific body part, system, or experience and can be represented in meditation in a variety of ways:

- **EARTH:** Associated with the weight and solidity of the body, represented by crystals or plants.
- **FIRE:** Associated with the temperature of the body, represented by candles or incense.
- **AIR:** Associated with the continuous breath and oxygen in the body, represented by wind chimes or a fan.
- **WATER:** Associated with all the liquids in the body, represented by shells or water in a bowl.
- **SPACE:** Associated with all human experience that is not tangible, represented by a bell or singing bowl.

THE FIFTH ELEMENT

Space—sometimes referred to as "ether"—originates from the Latin root *aether*, which refers to a pure bright upper air of the sky. In ancient Greek mythology, this element was considered a pure substance that only the gods breathed. Today, it is often used in a figurative sense, referring to the unknown and, in meditation, it can relate to space, intuition, the spirit, experiences, and stillness.

HOW TO INCORPORATE THE ELEMENTS

Incorporate fire into your meditation when you feel heated or need an energetic spark. Trataka meditation, meaning to gaze or to look in Sanskrit, is a practice that involves staring at a single point—commonly, a flame. Often called "candle gazing," this powerful practice is most effective when done after sunset or before sunrise with your kit's tealight.

BENEFITS
Promotes concentration, improves memory, and channels spiritual awareness.

HOW TO PRACTICE TRATAKA MEDITATION:
- Find a dark place where you can be comfortably seated and position your candle at eye level.
- Before lighting the candle, take a long cooling breath in and release a warming exhale.
- Light the candle and, when it is safe to do so, close your eyes and let your breath resume its natural rhythm.
- Once you are tuned into your breath, open your eyes and gently gaze at the center of the candle flame without blinking for as long as possible, without straining.
- Close your eyes when there is an urge to blink and try to keep the afterimage of the flame burning bright. If there is no afterimage, visualize the flame in your mind's eye.
- When the image of the flame dims, open your eyes and repeat this unblinking gaze and resting of your eyes for however long it feels comfortable.
- Close the practice with a deep breath from the diaphragm where the solar plexus chakra (associated with fire) is located, and speak the solar plexus mantra:

Ram

Do not practice trataka for more than 10 minutes at a time, especially if you are using a candle. Trataka should not be practiced daily, or a two-week break should be taken at least every 2 months, to avoid any retinal damage that may occur by staring at a flame for prolonged periods of time. This practice is contraindicated if you have cataracts, myopia, glaucoma, astigmatism, or epilepsy.

MEDITATION | Incorporating the Elements

MEDITATION CARDS

MEDITATION | Meditation Cards

WHAT ARE MEDITATION CARDS?

Make meditation a part of your daily routine and long-term lifestyle with the help of meditation cards. The meditation cards in this kit provide a varied selection of activities and challenges to be enjoyed every day and keep you encouraged and engaged on your mindfulness journey. Find out the different ways each of the 45 meditation cards can work best for you by exploring each card group, easily identified by the colors on the back of each card.

GREEN CARDS: YOGA

There are 10 yoga cards with simple, mindful yoga poses to complement any meditation practice. These cards can also help the user to bring awareness to the body and quiet the mind by promoting a calm physical focus.

PINK CARDS: TIMING

Each of the 5 timing cards features a different timescale, ranging from 1 to 30 minutes, to help you set challenges and experiment with your practice. Reset your mind in minutes with mini meditations and delve deeper into the present with longer ones.

BLUE CARDS: AFFIRMATIONS AND ACTIVITIES

The 30 affirmation and activity cards provide exercises to enhance your meditation practice. Discover a new favorite mantra to motivate your meditation or bring lightness into your day with a refreshing breathing exercise.

HOW TO USE YOUR MEDITATION CARDS

Instill a dose of determination into your practice by selecting a meditation card daily. Doing so will bring consistency to your meditation routine and perseverance to your practice.

MEDITATION REMINDER

Keep your deck of meditation cards on your desk or by your bed as a reminder to draw from them every day. Keep your selected card on display where you will see it regularly or on your person, in a bag or pocket, to act as a useful reminder to indulge in regular moments of meditation.

MIXING CARDS

One way to select a daily card is to mix up all three card categories into one deck and choose a card at random. This intriguing exercise could open your practice up to new possibilities and provide an unexpected yoga pose or refreshing new breathing exercise.

CONSCIOUS CHOOSING

Bring awareness into your daily card selection by considering your needs or intentions for that day as you shuffle the deck of meditation cards. You may want to close your eyes and bring attention to your breath as you shuffle to help you concentrate on your intention.

REPEATED CARDS

If you keep drawing the same card, you might be tempted to pick another, however, there is no harm in revisiting practices. As you find your mood and needs change daily, you'll discover how you engage with a previously explored practice, pose, or timing may also change.

MEDITATION | Meditation Cards

Add spontaneity into your practice and avoid any meditation from becoming monotonous with the different potential card combinations available. Combine the meditation cards and create new practices to enjoy daily.

HOW TO COMBINE THE CARDS:
- Separate the cards into their three groups of timing, yoga, and activities, (easily identified by their different colors). This way, you have the option to choose one of each card "type."
- Alternatively, you can skip the first step and combine the cards more freely, perhaps selecting an activity card with two timing cards to combine for a longer practice.
- Next, create a 2- or 3-card combination. There is no right or wrong way to go about selecting your combination. You may want to choose 1 card from each category, or you may want to practice without a time limit.
- Once you become more confident with the cards, you can also try creating combinations of more than 3, perhaps having a sequence of yoga pose cards with a different timing for each and closing with a breathing exercise or mantra with an activity card.
- If you find a combination of cards that you did or did not enjoy, keep the same yoga and/or activity card(s) out for the next day's practice and draw a different timing card to see how time can bring a change of perspective and create a different experience.

COMBINING MEDITATION AND YOGA

Let your mind rest and your body take the lead with the mindful movements of yoga. Meditating with yoga involves cultivating an awareness of how your body feels without casting judgment. There are no rules about how yoga meditation should feel, so long as it feels right to you.

YOGA POSES:

- **STANDING:** Mountain and warrior pose help bring a warm and wakeful energy to a practice, so are good to incorporate into a morning meditation and at the beginning of any longer sequence of yoga poses.
- **BALANCING:** Tree and plank pose bring a greater focus to meditation as they require higher levels of concentration. They can also highlight areas of your body that require your attention, so should be adopted with gentle patience.
- **SEATED:** Lotus and cobbler's pose provide a calm and heightened awareness. Seated poses often require more effort than they look so are suited to the end of a meditation practice when your body is warmer.
- **RESTING:** Corpse and child's pose encourage rest and are the perfect way to take restorative breaks within meditation or as a closing pose to enjoy a final moment of relaxation.

YOGA CARDS

The yoga cards can be mixed up for a surprise pose in each meditation session or selected specifically to suit your practice. Select one card initially and build up toward trying a sequence of yoga poses. Combining yoga and meditation should be a challenge but never a competition, so keep within the limits of your body.

MEDITATION | Meditation Cards

BENEFITS
Promotes awareness, improves wellbeing, and channels strength.

HOW TO PRACTICE YOGA WITH MEDITATION:
- Select a yoga card at random or one that fits your mood.
- Take some time to set up your space with any supports, blankets, or cushions that will help you meditate as comfortably as possible.
- When ready, adopt the yoga pose, taking a moment to shuffle and shift as much as needed before you find some stillness in the pose.
- Take your attention to your thoughts. First, simply let them pass through you, letting them be without analysis, before directing your awareness away from your mind and toward your body.
- Focus on one body part at a time. As you bring awareness to each body part, you will likely feel it automatically soften under your mental gaze. Tension often collects in the neck and shoulders, so take extra time on this area.
- If you feel any lingering tension, stay with that area of your body. Focus on letting go of any discomfort that you can and accepting any discomfort that you cannot control.
- Recognize your body's limits and let that dictate how long to stay in any given yoga pose.
- When a pose is no longer serving you, gently move into another or complete your practice by bringing your hands together in prayer and honoring your dedication to your meditation by speaking the Sanskrit greeting:

Namaste

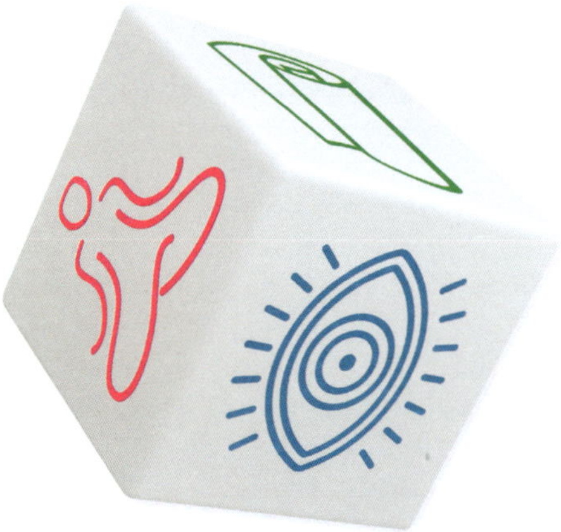

MEDITATION DICE

WHAT ARE MEDITATION DICE?

Meditation dice are fun, useful tools to keep your meditation practice interesting. Included in your kit is a six-sided meditation dice that displays a symbol on each side. Each symbol on the dice corresponds with a different page of the book that contains step-by-step instructions for a meditation practice, including body scan, movement, mantra, breath awareness, noting, and visualization. The dice allows you to select a random meditation practice every day to inspire new opportunities and ways to meditate.

HOW TO USE:
Simply roll the dice and locate the page in the book with the same symbol at the top to find your next meditation inspiration. Use the dice on its own or alongside the meditation cards for a new challenge.

HOW TO COMBINE WITH THE CARDS:
To use in combination with the meditation cards, roll the dice and . . .

- choose a timing card and complete the meditation on the dice for that allotted time.
- choose a yoga card and incorporate the position into the meditation shown on the dice.
- choose an activity card and combine the mantra or breathing exercise on the card with the dice meditation.
- choose a card from two or more categories and blend them with the dice meditation for a full practice shake-up!

HOW TO USE MEDITATION DICE

Take overthinking which meditation practice to choose next out of the equation and leave it in the hands of your kit's meditation dice. Let your dice do the decision-making and take a chance on one of the following six potential practices:

- **BODY SCAN:** Also known as Vipassana, this popular relaxation practice involves bringing awareness to the body, one part at a time, from head to toe.
- **NOTING:** Also known as mindfulness meditation, noting is a simple practice of acceptance that involves gently taking notice of a thought as it pops into your head before letting it go.
- **VISUALIZATION:** A creative type of meditation where a person imagines a mental image or scenario to help channel a desired outcome such as peace or inspiration.
- **MOVEMENT:** Any form of meditation that incorporates moving the body, movement meditation focuses the mind on how the body feels in the present moment.
- **BREATH AWARENESS:** Mindful breathing that focuses on bringing awareness to the breath, it is known for improving concentration and easing anxiety.
- **MANTRA:** Usually a short phrase or word that is repeated to bring a person confidence or a sense of spiritual power or peace, mantra meditation can bring a focused awareness to a meditation.

MEDITATION | Meditation Dice

MEDITATION DICE PRACTICES

VIPASSANA (BODY SCAN)

Vipassana (or body scan) is a mindfulness practice that involves scanning your body for pain, tension or anything out of the ordinary. By connecting more with our physical bodies, we aim to create a deeper connection to our emotional selves, also.

BENEFITS
Promotes relaxation, improves sleep, and channels empathy.

HOW TO PRACTICE VIPASSANA MEDITATION:
- Take a deep breath in, letting it fill your entire body before releasing it.
- Let your body become heavy and gently sink into your surroundings—your head into a pillow or your back against a chair.
- Starting at the head, bring awareness to each specific area—forehead, eyelids, jaw, etc.—and notice how they feel. If there is any tension, consciously release it before moving on to the next body part.
- Continue to scan down through your body, noticing and relaxing each part.
- If your mind wanders, acknowledge the distraction before moving your attention back to your body.
- As you reach the tips of your toes, notice the pleasant heaviness tugging your body into rest.
- Draw a deep breath in and release any lingering tension from your entire body on your exhale.
- If needed, wake your body back up gently, starting by wriggling the hands and feet to move energy back through your body, opening your eyes last.

NOTING MEDITATION

Noting, or mindfulness meditation, is a simple practice that involves gently giving a name to a thought as it pops into your head before letting it go. Open your mind to thoughts that you have been closed off to and get ready to clear some mental space with this visualization meditation.

BENEFITS
Promotes awareness, improves focus, and channels acceptance.

HOW TO PRACTICE NOTING MEDITATION:

- Make yourself comfortable and find a position that feels good in this moment, however that looks to you.
- Practice bringing your entire focus to your breath, noticing the coolness of your inhale and warmth of your exhale and allow it to anchor you in the present.
- As thoughts arise, begin to label them. Start very simply by noting every thought as a "thought" in your mind.
- As you observe each thought and grow used to the practice, begin to be more specific, i.e., if you think about work, label it "work," if you think about family, label it "family."
- Next, try to label the emotions behind each thought as "positive," "negative," or "neutral." Touch base with your anchoring breath if emotions begin to eclipse the thought.
- Remind yourself that every thought is a temporary visitor. If a thought is a welcome guest, embrace it for as long as it feels good to do so. If a thought is an unwelcome visitor, visualize opening a door and, on each exhale, encourage the thought to exit through it.
- Ground yourself back into your surroundings by taking note of each sense before closing the practice—and door—with a loving breath.

VISUALIZATION MEDITATION

Visualization meditation creates a soft landing place for your mind to rest. It also provides a soothing distraction to keep your mind from becoming fixated on negative thoughts. Visualization can also be used to cultivate certain psychological qualities, such as acceptance, gratitude, or motivation. Great for distracted or anxious minds, focusing on an imagined setting can soothe stresses and encourage a clearer and more positive mindset.

BENEFITS
Promotes calmness, improves creativity, and channels intentions.

HOW TO PRACTICE VISUALIZATION TO CULTIVATE GRATITUDE:
- Close your eyes to minimize distractions and inhale deeply. Exhale with an audible sigh and let your breath return to its natural, easy rhythm.
- Begin to visualize all the parts of your day that you are grateful for. These can be big or small, from your first sip of coffee to sitting in a favorite chair. If you cannot visualize in your mind's eye, list all the elements of your chosen scenario one by one and mentally describe them to yourself in detail to conjure up a sense of place.
- If your day has been bad, your mind may wander away from the positive and fixate on the negative. It is fine if this happens; simply take awareness back to your breath before returning to your gratitude list.
- When you reach the end of your gratitude list, complete your meditation with a mantra:

Inhale love, exhale love

MOVEMENT MEDITATION

When you struggle to be still, take your meditation on the move with a walk. Movement meditation helps achieve mindfulness by switching from thinking to experiencing. A walk in the city can be just as mindful as a walk in nature if you engage with the moment with an open-hearted awareness. Begin your day with a walking meditation and try it in all different weathers to fully wake up the senses.

BENEFITS
Lowers stress levels, improves physical health, and regulates emotions.

HOW TO PRACTICE MOVEMENT MEDITATION:
- Begin your walk without a clear destination in mind to allow you to connect with the present. If walking is not an option for you physically, try this exercise as a visualization meditation instead.
- Begin by observing the movement of your body. Notice how it is not just the legs that are moving, but the arms swaying, the eyes blinking, and the feet flexing.
- Take your attention to internal observations. Feel a warmth from within rise to the surface of the skin and notice your muscles contracting and relaxing with each step.
- Expand your observations to the external and take in the sounds, smells, sights, feel, and space around you. Try to observe them all, the good, the bad, and the smelly, without judgment.
- Move within the moment, noticing thoughts pass through your mind as your body passes through the environment.
- Stay with this practice for as long as it feels good or for however long makes sense.

BREATH AWARENESS MEDITATION

Breathwork is the cornerstone of meditation, grounding you in the present and connecting you with how you feel within it. Breath awareness focuses on mindful breathing and can improve concentration while reducing stress and anxiety. Try the breath awareness meditation below to bring clarity to a scattered or stressed mind.

BENEFITS
Promotes calmness, improves concentration, and reduces anxiety.

HOW TO PRACTICE BREATH AWARENESS MEDITATION:
- Begin by taking a long and well-deserved breath in through your nose and an even longer exhale out through your mouth.
- Now, without changing your breathing pattern, take your attention to a part of your body where you notice your breath—maybe your chest rising and falling or the air traveling through your nose. Give this area of your body your full attention and let it be your anchor in this meditation. Take in all the sensations of breathing in and out, noticing the feel of your ribcage expanding or the coolness of air entering your nose.
- If your attention veers off track, point it back to your anchor point and your breath flowing freely through it. The breath is an unlimited meditation tool, so treat every new breath as a clean slate.
- Close your meditation by taking a deep breath in and exhaling it completely.
- If they have been closed, gently open your eyes and bring your surroundings into focus one object at a time, slowly grounding yourself back into your day with a calmer focus.

MANTRA MEDITATION

Mantra meditation is more than just words. From writing your own to learning sacred Sanskrit sounds, mantras bring clear intention into any meditation and can help actualize goals and overcome challenges. Typically involving saying a word or short phrase aloud, adding an empowering mantra into your practice is an energizing way to hone awareness, prepare for a big day, and become more mindful in minutes.

BENEFITS
Promotes good self-esteem, improves confidence, and channels strong intentions.

HOW TO PRACTICE MANTRA MEDITATION:
- Consider your intentions and choose a fitting mantra or affirmation. This may be one of your own creation, such as an "I Am . . ." affirmation where you add a desired or observed quality. Alternatively, if selecting a mantra in Sanskrit, make sure to understand its meaning and channel this meaning as you chant it.
- Bring awareness to your breath without changing its rhythm and notice the sound of your exhale and inhale.
- With arms outstretched and face tilted toward the sky, begin to speak your chosen mantra or affirmation in a style that feels right to you, such as singing, chanting, whispering, or syncing it with your breath.
- Meditate for as long as it takes for the message of your words to truly sink in, or for as long as it feels good or natural to do so.
- Complete your practice with a deep breath in, filling yourself with gratitude for taking the time to practice today, and exhale slow and steady, ready to start anew.

MEDITATION MASTER

MEDITATION | Meditation Master

MORE MEDITATIONS

Well-versed in visualization and no longer a beginner in breathwork. This next chapter will have you mastering the art of meditation through more advanced practices. Aiming to elevate your awareness and fine-tune your focus, explore these more challenging exercises with an open heart and a willingness to begin again whenever the present escapes you. If you find yourself struggling with any of the following meditations, revisit some of the earlier techniques covered.

REFLECTION MEDITATION: A dedicated practice centered around introspection and inner understanding. This meditation relies on a connection to your body and draws on techniques such as noting.

LOVING KINDNESS: A challenging practice to mend past relations and present-day anxieties. This meditation draws upon calming breathwork and visualization techniques.

SPIRITUAL: A practice that helps unite you with the greater world using elemental connections and breathwork. Review the breath awareness and elements meditations to prepare for this practice.

CHAKRA: A creative and spiritual exploration into the Sanskrit energy chakra centers. Visualization and knowledge of crystals are valuable skills to bring to this meditation.

NEED MORE HELP?

Remember, the meditation tools such as the cards, dice, candle, and clear quartz crystal used earlier in this book can all be incorporated into these more challenging practices to enhance meditations and support your journey further.

REFLECTION MEDITATION

This meditation comes from the inward belief that we should mindfully focus on the present. Developing a mindful brain can help us to remain grounded in the present and focus on what really matters in life instead of becoming lost in the past.

BENEFITS

Helps you to build structure, keep sight of the future, and become a positive influence

HOW TO PRACTICE REFLECTION MEDITATION:

- Begin by finding a comfortable position and taking a seat. Then, close your eyes and take several deep breaths.
- Continue to take deep breaths and pay attention to your body while doing so. Ask yourself these questions: How are you feeling? Do you feel open and relaxed or heavy and tight? Are your breaths coming easily?
- The goal with this meditation is to pay attention to how your body feels in the moment. By noticing physical cues, you can help bring yourself into the current moment and recognize your emotions and thoughts.
- If any unwanted thoughts come to mind, don't bat them away but instead try to understand where the thought came from. If the thought bothers you, you may choose to let it go and re-ground yourself back into the moment by once again focusing on your body and how you are feeling, helping to bring you back to peace.

MEDITATION | Meditation Master

MEDITATION FOR ANXIETY

Most meditation practices will soothe anxiety but maybe none more so than the ultimate self-care practice of a loving kindness meditation. Combine this practice with the calming 3-3-3 breathing exercise to say goodbye to stress and hello to harmony.

BENEFITS

Promotes self-love, improves peace, and channels forgiveness.

HOW TO PRACTICE A LOVING KINDNESS MEDITATION:

- Settle into a comfortable position and begin your practice with a soothing 3-3-3 breathing exercise, inhaling for 3 seconds, gently pausing your breath for 3 seconds, and exhaling for 3 more seconds.
- Now, think about someone who you love. Whether that someone is a friend, partner, parent, or a pet, hold them in your mind and visualize their face at peace as you send loving kindness to them.
- Next, think about someone who you have not seen or thought of in a while and extend the same loving kindness to them. Again, visualize their face being at peace as you think of them with kindness.
- Now, extend this kindness even further to someone you may have once felt dislike towards (or they toward you). If negative thoughts of the person spring to mind, let them appear, observe them as old feelings, and replace them with this present state of kindness. Holding onto hate damages your peace and so, by extending kindness to your enemies, you are also extending it to yourself.
- Lastly, bring your awareness back to yourself, in mind, body, and spirit and visualize your face becoming at peace.

MEDITATION | Meditation Master

SPIRITUAL MEDITATION

Spiritual meditation can be used to discover and rediscover your sense of self and place in the world, no matter your culture or personal belief system. Explore a deeper connection to the outside world and reconnect with yourself by connecting with your breath in this deeply personal and adaptable meditation.

BENEFITS
Promotes breath awareness, improves connection, and channels inner bliss.

HOW TO PRACTICE SPIRITUAL MEDITATION:
- Start by sitting comfortably in a relaxed but upright position. Place one hand over your heart and the other hand over your stomach.
- Take a moment to register the natural rhythm of your breath and appreciate it as the essential life source that it is.
- Once you have tapped into your breath, focus on breathing deep into your stomach from your diaphragm. Notice your hand on your stomach moving in and out with your breath.
- Begin to quietly hum to generate a little warmth in the mouth and wake up the vocal cords.
- Speak the Sanskrit *So Ham* mantra, meaning I Am (That), also known as the mantra of the breath. Listen for the *So* sound as you inhale and the *Ham* as you exhale.
- Alternatively, if you have a mantra that suits your spiritual beliefs, you may prefer to use that, but make sure you connect it to your breath.
- Repeat the mantra for as long as you like, and revisit it throughout the day whenever you need a top-up of spiritual bliss.

CHAKRA MEDITATION

Stemming from ancient Sanskrit beliefs, "chakra" broadly translates to "spinning wheel" and refers to spiritual energy centers within the body. The seven chakras commonly observed in meditation are found on the opposite page.

BENEFITS
Promotes healing, improves wellbeing, and channels inner peace.

HOW TO PRACTICE CHAKRA MEDITATION:
- Familiarize yourself with the seven chakras and their associated body areas, colors, and attributes.
- Find a comfortable seated or lying position where your chakras are aligned.
- Travel through the chakras one at a time like you would with a body scan meditation (see page 45) from the root to the crown.
- At each chakra, pause and observe any tension in that area of your body.
- Visualize each chakra area flooding with its associated color and flushing out any discomfort until your entire self is flooded in a healing rainbow of color.
- Variations: Try the same meditation using the associated crystals or mantras on the activity meditation cards.

THE SEVEN CHAKRAS

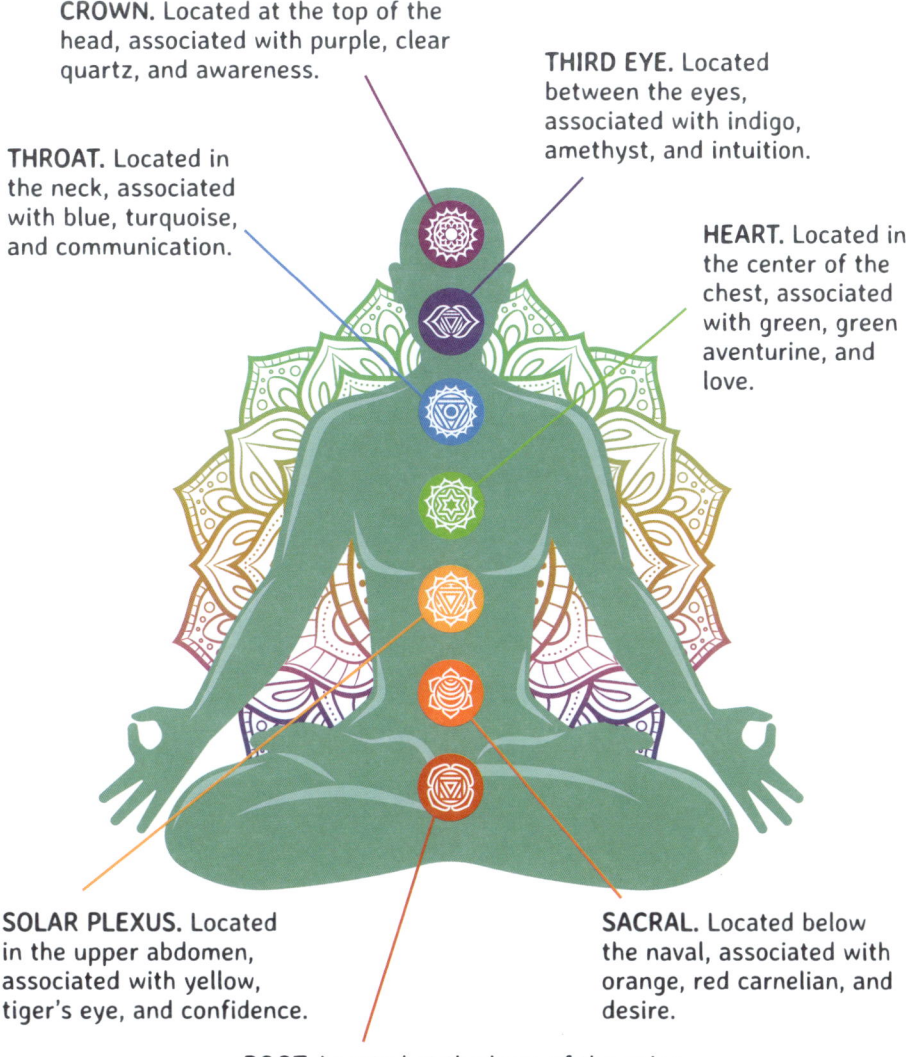

CROWN. Located at the top of the head, associated with purple, clear quartz, and awareness.

THIRD EYE. Located between the eyes, associated with indigo, amethyst, and intuition.

THROAT. Located in the neck, associated with blue, turquoise, and communication.

HEART. Located in the center of the chest, associated with green, green aventurine, and love.

SOLAR PLEXUS. Located in the upper abdomen, associated with yellow, tiger's eye, and confidence.

SACRAL. Located below the naval, associated with orange, red carnelian, and desire.

ROOT. Located at the base of the spine, associated with red, red jasper, and stability.

HOW TO STAY MOTIVATED

When you lack the motivation to meditate and your cup is feeling empty, consider what it needs to be filled with.

A dose of concentration?

An expansion of compassion?

A full body relaxation?

Avoid getting stuck in a practice that is no longer serving you. As your needs change, so should your meditation. If at any point you begin to feel unmotivated with meditation, take a break from what you have been practicing and try something new. What worked yesterday might not work today, so explore as many avenues as you like to get to where you want to go.

MEDITATION MOTIVATORS:

- **ENERGIZER:** Low energy levels can result in a lack of focus and interest so try doing some energizing breathwork such as belly breathing before meditating and you'll find your practice is instantly refreshed.
- **TARGETS:** Setting a target for your meditation can help you stick to a dedicated routine. Try meditating every day for a week, or challenge yourself to increase your meditation practice by one minute every day for a month.
- **MEDITATION TOOLS:** You are only ever a roll of the dice or draw of a card away from meditation inspiration, so remember to regularly utilize the tools included in this kit.

GOING FURTHER

MEDITATION | Going Further

Now is the time to trust your inner voice and continue with the practices that have worked for you. Keep this guide nearby for reference as you establish a regular meditation routine. Eventually, favored practices will become second nature and never feel further than a mindful breath away.

Nothing needs to be set in stone, so keep your mind open and your practice fluid. A body scan might be the ideal tonic after a physical or tense day, or a peaceful visualization meditation session may be the missing inner peace of today's puzzle. What's worked for you before may not be what you need in the present.

Meditation doesn't need to be a solo activity. Meditating with family and friends is a great way to stay motivated and regularly keep up with your practice. Chanting in group settings can amp up mantra meditation and walking with a fellow meditator could lead to new destinations on your movement meditation journey.

If you are still looking for your perfect meditation match, keep exploring with an open-hearted awareness. No time in meditation or working toward a meditative state is ever wasted. A meditation where you have had to return your thoughts to the present 10 times is just as valuable as a practice where you have had to do it 100 times. Perfection is never the goal for any meditation practice, only progress.

GLOSSARY

Affirmation
A positive statement of intent that is directed toward yourself to offer emotional support and encouragement.

Anchor
A meditation device that helps ground yourself and steer wandering thoughts back to the present—an anchor could be an object, sensation, activity, or anything else that grounds you to the present.

Breathwork
Any conscious and controlled breathing technique or exercise that is often used for relaxation, therapeutic, and meditation purposes.

Body scan
A meditation practice, also known as Vipassana, that involves methodically bringing awareness to each body part, from head to toe, observing any tension, pain, or sensation in the body and mind.

Chakra
An internal spinning energy center within the body that is connected to a person's physical, mental, and spiritual wellbeing, relating to an ancient Sanskrit belief.

Crystal
A substance made of a repeated geometric pattern, often angular and sparkling in appearance, and used in many alternative therapies.

Mantra
Often a short phrase or word that is repeated to bring a person confidence or a sense of spiritual power or peace, traditionally used in Hinduism and Buddhism.

Meditation
The mindful practice of engaging with the present in a dedicated moment of reflection and contemplation.

Mindfulness
A practice that involves becoming aware of the present moment.

Noting
A meditation practice, sometimes called mindfulness meditation, that involves gently observing and releasing thoughts.

Reflection Meditation
A meditation that stems from the inward belief that we should mindfully focus on the present.

Sanskrit
An ancient language belonging to the Indo-Aryan group that is rooted in Hinduism and many Indian languages.

Trataka
A meditation practice that involves staring at a single point, commonly, a flame.

Visualization
The act of picturing a positive image or idea that is often practiced to help calm or focus the mind and body.